A Walk in Our Shoes

Poems of Enlightenment

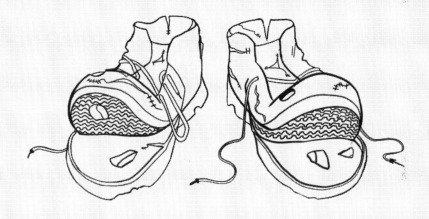

By Patricia Middleton

Cover by Leena Shariq

Thank you momma and daddy.
Dorothy Middleton and James Benjamin Middleton

Thank You God.

Author/Publisher: Patricia Middleton
ISBN-979-8-218-14251-3
Text Copyright 2022

A Walk in Our Shoes/Written by Patricia Middleton
Cover by Leena Shariq

Printed in the United States of America.

Dedications

This book is dedicated to my brother Anthony Middleton, my cousins Duane and Ira Manigault, Marion Jenkins and Kent Holliday.

This book is also dedicated to the Ancestors who bared the burden of slavery, all who marched and fought for civil rights in the 1950's and 60's, the Black Lives Matter Movement, every organization and every individual who fought and continue to fight for equal rights for Blacks and all other races that face discrimination.

INTRODUCTION

No one knows the pain and anguish of Black folk like Black folk. There is not a day that goes by that there is not some incident, whether personal or in the news, that we are all negatively reminded of the color of our skin.

It is ironic that our ancestors were brought here on slave ships by the ancestors of the same people who tell us to, "go back where you came from."

Our ancestors worked in the scorching sun all day tending crops with little food, rest or pay. They were sold like cattle and beat unmercifully, as if they were clad with armor. And even though Blacks literally built this country, that made White America wealthy, Black people were left poor and destitute. What happened to their 40 acres and a mule, a tool box and fifty dollars?

Four hundred years of slavery, and that wasn't enough. We currently experience every form of discrimination imaginable; higher unemployment rates, lower pay, substandard housing, non-lending practices, bogus convictions, police brutality and deaths (George Floyd, Breonna Taylor, Ahmaud Arbery and so many others), to name a few. And after decades dealing with this mistreatment, some White people are still questioning the validity of inequality in America when we are still dealing with racial divide.

White people! When are you going to stop acting like an ostrich, and take your heads out of the sand and stand up and do your part to help end racism and discrimination? Where is the larger number of you who know that it is wrong and won't speak out about it? What does that say about you?

We are still dealing with voter rights issues. How do you have people in Congress that are supposed to fairly represent the interests of every American citizen and they have to consistently visit the 15th Amendment to the Constitution every few years to rule on laws that should have already been put in place to protect everyone's right to vote.

These poems are not about hating White people. All White people are not racist. I stated in the beginning of the book that it is a book about those to whom it applies. If it doesn't apply to you, then there is no need to own it.

This is a book of poems about our struggles that seem to fall on deaf ears across America. It is a book of enlightening some in the White race and some in the Black race of the systemic racism that exists in America.

There is still a lot that Black children need to learn about their own history. Black History is celebrated and observed in the month of February because the history of Blacks have been ignored over the ages.

There is now the issue of not wanting to teach the complete history of America in our school systems, especially when it relates to slavery and what constituted bringing Africans from their continent. People need to know the complete history of the slave trade and what happened to slaves while living on the plantations. White people never hesitate talking about the Civil War and waving their flags. Slavery had a part in the war. You can't talk about one without talking about the other.

How do you block out critical times in history that helped shape this nation? The excuse has been that you don't want White children to feel guilty about what happened during slavery. The truth is that you don't want White children to know the truth about the unthinkable atrocities their ancestors committed against Blacks.

No one should be able to block out the truths of history for any reason. There should not be a division of which history is more important to teach or learn than the other. History is history.

This book is about those to whom it applies.

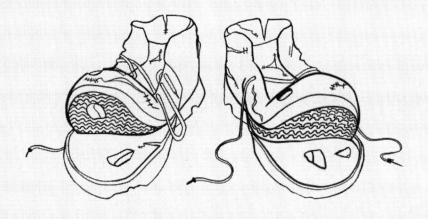

A Walk in Our Shoes

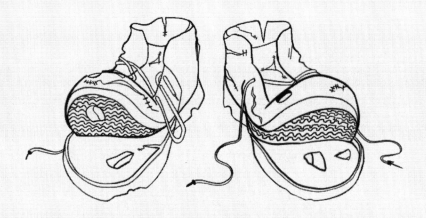

How Do You Do It?

How do you look a man in his eyes,

and then take his children away?

How do you rape his mother and wife,

and think that it's okay?

How do you relinquish him of his pride,

and expect him to look the other way?

How do you beat him to the ground with a whip,

and expect him to work in the fields all day?

How do you look yourself in the mirror,

and continue to carry on this way?

It comes easy to those who have hearts of stone,

and who can take real history away.

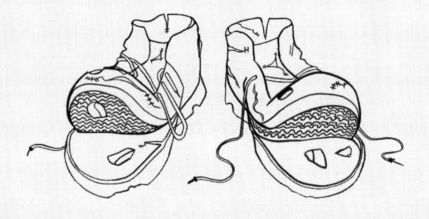

Fighting for the Right to be "White"
(Insurrectionist Ode to Donald Trump)

Storming the Capital with your big guns,

as if nothing would be said.

If Black men had done that exact same thing, they would

absolutely be dead.

Where is Trump, your Great White Hope, who left you

hanging by a thread?

He's at home every night sleeping comfortably in his Mar-

a-Lago bed.

And you are in deep trouble with the law because you

were egregiously misled.

Politicians don't have you on their minds, yet you

constantly have them in your head.

As if they are really going to do something for you, they

just let the rich get richer instead.

What is it going to take for you to understand and open up

your minds?

Black people are not your enemy.

We are all being left behind.

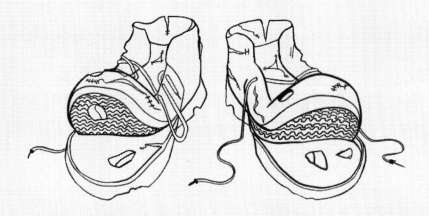

Go Back Where You Came From

Go back where you came from.
That should apply to most people you see.

But every time you say it, it is almost always directed at people
of color like me.

Do you not know your history? Do you think it's a mistake?
Take the risk of reading all about it so you won't think it's fake.

Race was invented by a Caucasian human being,
and had people separated by class,

for two simple reasons, so he could make plenty of money at
our expense and sit on his privileged white ass.

If anybody should leave here, it should be you.
We aren't the only ones who came across the sea, you came
across the sea too.

The only difference in our journey is that we were shackled in
two by two.

We built this country sun up and sun down,
how dare you try and send us away,

If anyone should stay in this country
it's the Indians you tried to kill

and those you put on reservations and tucked away.

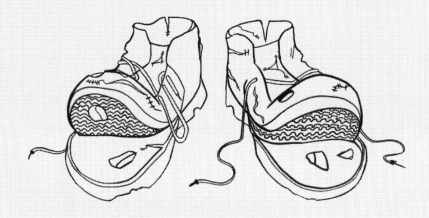

Indigo, Indigo Where Did You Go?

Indigo, Indigo, where did you go?
I went to South Carolina to a town called Pocataligo.

I was one of South Carolina's most valuable crops,
and made it all the way up the chain next to rice,
where I was second from the top.

Using the labor of slaves who came long before me,
who toiled with the grueling step by step process
that created me from the leaves of a tropical tree.

My color of deep shades of deep violet and blue,
was mentioned in several Bible verses and was
popular among royalty too.

The slaves who worked hard and long on my crops,
worked in the fields all day, but it all went to the top.

Once again intense slave labor served them well,
profiting from several products made eventually
in Britain as well.

Indigo, indigo where do you be?
I be in the jeans of every man and woman you see.

(The slaves wore jeans long before they became popular and profitable among white
designers who capitalized greatly in the fashion world.)

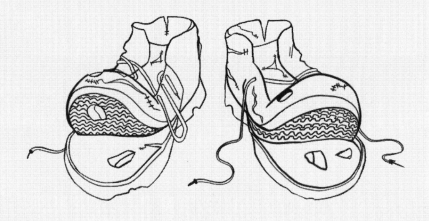

I'm Trying to Understand

You didn't like our big lips,

but now you inject yours as big as you can.

You didn't like our dark skin,

but you stay in the sun to get tan.

You didn't like our big hips,

but now you pay for a plastic surgeon to

enlarge your can.

What is this all about? I'm trying to

understand.

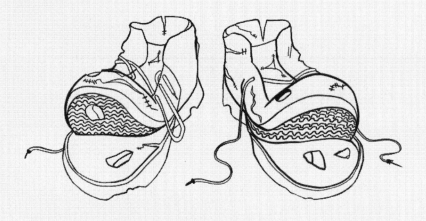

We Will Wear Our Hair

Dreads, braids, afros are the hairstyles

of our kings and queens.

These are the natural roots of strength like

Sampson

and that of Black human beings.

Who are you to say what hairstyles we adorn?

Our hair has been naturally kinky ever since we

were born.

Our race has made so many sacrifices, hair being

only one.

We will continue to wear our hair natural and

wear it natural till our day is done.

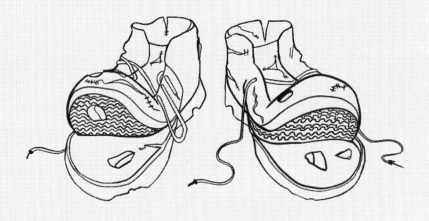

White Privilege

You are immune to every situation around you,
unlimited opportunities are always at your door.

Power and money have been your compass, as you
always try to gain even more.

You started out as the Black man's Master,
and then try to act like you don't understand,

that he's always had a disadvantage,
because at one time you considered him
to be three fifths of a man.

The Black man pulled himself up
by his bootstraps
all the way up from the floor.
Even though he struggled emotionally,
he always went back for more.

We all know the playing field has never been even,
and the Black man, seldom had
the opportunity to win.

If you don't believe what I said,
change the color of your skin.
You'll never, ever, ever get to have
White privilege again.

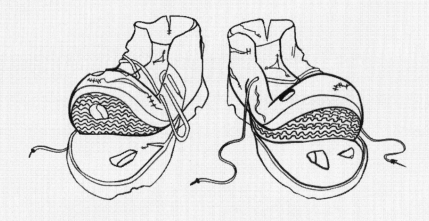

Infamous Karens

Karens here. Karens there. There are Karens everywhere.

Whenever we think that things are okay,

here comes a Karen that demands people of color listen to what she has to say.

And even more, she demands that they have to obey.

She lets them know where they deserve or have a right to be.

She even tells them to go back to their own countries.

How does that brazen behavior come to be?

She has a sense of entitlement but she doesn't have a clue about my or her own history.

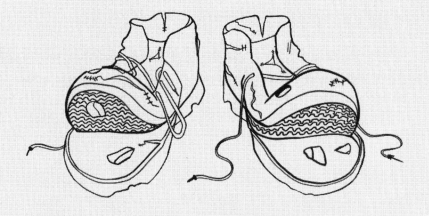

ENTITLEMENT

ENTITLEMENT

ENTITLEMENT

ENTITLEMENT

ENTITLEMENT

ENTITLEMENT

ENTITLEMENT

ENTITLEMENT

ENTITLEMENT

ENTITLEMENT

ENTITLEMENT

ENTITLEMENT

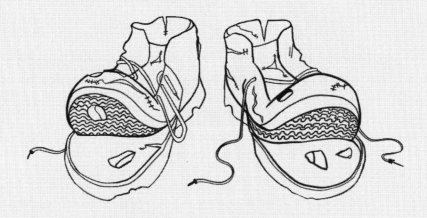

The Word Nigger

No matter where it came from,

or how it came to be.

It doesn't matter how some young Black

youth categorize it.

It will always have a negative connotation to

my ancestors who struggled

and died to be free.

Heard from the mouths of White folk,

before, during and after hanging

a Black man from a tree.

Calling Black people nigger

only clarifies who you really want to be.

It comes from the teachings of generations

of your ancestors,

and for some will be ingrained in you

as your ancestors intended it to be.

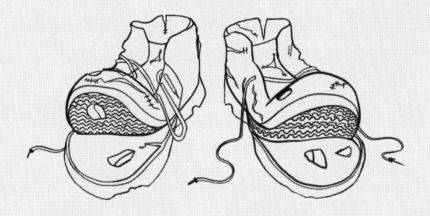

Crack Versus Powder Cocaine

Whether it be in powder,

or whether it be a rock.

The same jail or cell time should be given

for both versions equally on the clock.

Doctors, lawyers and everyone in between,

don't discriminate against the Black man

because he doesn't have any green.

One goes up the nose in powder, the other one

in the pipe and inhaled, in either case it doesn't

matter, equally both races need to go to jail.

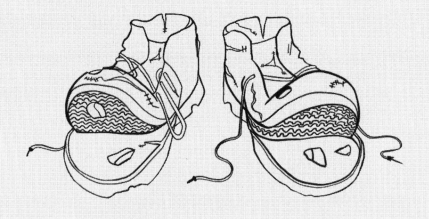

How Many More Times?

How many more times will you take a
Black man's life? How many more deaths
will it take?

How many more times does a Black man
have to try to plead for his life, while you
decide his fate?

What is it about him that scares you? What
does his dying gain?

Who taught you to have this evilness inside
you?

Can you even try to explain?

Does it not matter that the same blood you
bleed also runs through his veins?

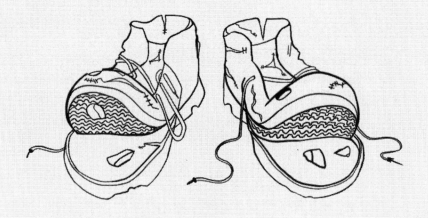

Will the Real Savages Please Stand Up?

You've called the American Indians savages and Black
men just the same, but you were the race that killed the
Indians, stole their land
and brought Blacks to America in chains.

You raped, beat, branded and worked us in sun
drenched fields all day.
And all we could do at night was to pray to God
that we would make it to see another day.

Even though we were called offensive things, and
physically treated with such vile and brutal hate,
with all the brutal atrocities delivered to us,
we still lead in being the most forgiving race
coming out of the gate.

Now most of your hate is suttle,
but sometimes you're so full of it you cannot hide,
like the distain you had for the election
of Barack Obama as president,
that a lot of you could not hide.
The scary part about it, is that you are in positions of
leadership for which our race has to rely.

Along came Donald Trump in office and without much
resistance,
he revealed and fueled an atmosphere of racial divide,
that had already existed.

On his watch thousands of people lost their lives to
Covid-19 every day.
It was over a million people that died
when it didn't have to be that way.

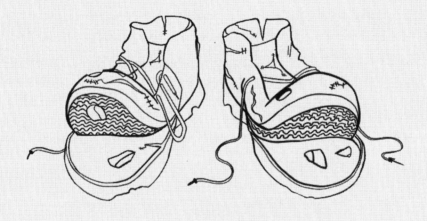

The People That Get Rescued

It appears that every person with an Anglo-Saxon face,

is able to come into the United States

without a hitch or their whereabouts being traced.

You sent away the Haitians after their brutal,

deadly earthquake.

Hispanics were sent back to threats of death,

put in cages and their children taken away.

The Ukrainians are welcomed with open arms,

with all out campaigns for help all over the place,

to help feed, cloth, shelter

and keep them in the U S of A.

Innocent Black men and boys

and sometimes women are killed by police

in America almost every day.

How many from your race protest out loud to keep this

from happening in any way?

But you will go to the ends of the earth

to put people who harm four legged animals away.

All of those forementioned need to be treated

the same way, with respect, kindness and love

that any decent and conscientious human being

should portray.

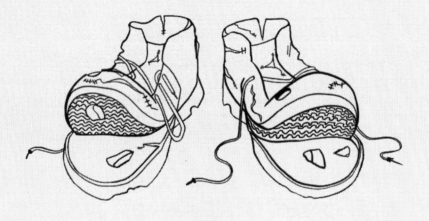

The United States of Whose America?

Whose America is this?
Certainly not to people of color like me.

When we have to revisit the voting rights act
year after year,
when we are supposed to be free.

You are killing our Black brothers and sisters,
picking them off one by one at alarming rates.

You will have to answer to God other than
yourselves,
but not at those Pearly gates.

Why are we still marching in order to be free?
We have just as much right
to be in this country,
as your race and every other
race has a right to be.

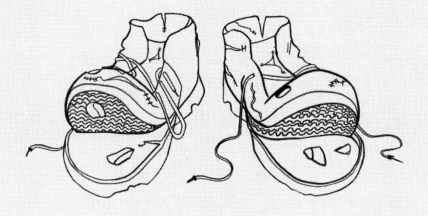

Black Lives Matter/
All Lives Matter

Black Lives Matter.

Brown Lives Matter.

Yellow Lives Matter.

White Lives Matter.

Black Lives Matter.

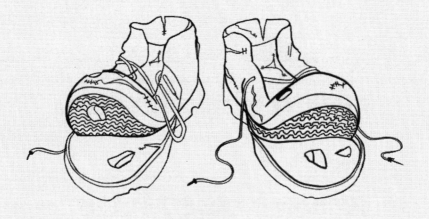

How Long Will It Be?

How long will it be

before you won't be able to corrupt

the minds of your children with prejudice

against those of a different race,

of those with a different face,

of those with different hair,

of those who you teach them to fear?

How long will it be, before they see and

fear who **you** really are?

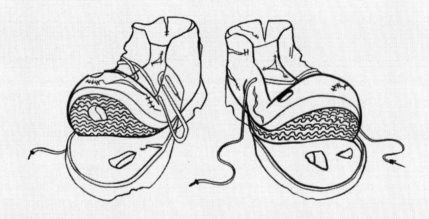

Final Call

We all have a common purpose. We all want to live in peace.

Let's destroy the prejudice now and let the hatred cease.

The world is looking at us every day and wondering

who we are.

Are we going to continue to teach the children to hate?

What happened to love conquers all?

Let's show compassion everywhere, no matter what the

color.

If we don't stop inflicting pain,

the destruction of the world will follow.

Made in the USA
Columbia, SC
18 August 2023

21764345R10028